Imagi

Moira Andrew

Imagine a Kiss

First Edition 2020

Published by Dempsey & Windle
15 Rosetrees
Guildford
Surrey
GU1 2HS
UK
01483 571164
dempseyandwindle.co.uk

A catalogue record for this book is available from the British Library.

ISBN: 978-1-913329-08-2

Moira Andrew was born and educated in Scotland. She has worked in most areas of primary education, as teacher, head teacher and college lecturer. She taught Creative Writing part-time in the University of Glamorgan. Moira has written a number of books on the creative arts for Belair, the most popular 'Language in Colour' and 'Paint a Poem'. She has seven poetry collections to her name, the most recent being 'Geese and Daughters' (IDP 2018) and 'Looking through Water' (Poetry Space 2020). Her collection for children 'Wish a Wish' was published by Poetry Space in 2012. Moira has written several reading books and edited numerous anthologies. Her work has been widely anthologised, performed live and broadcast on the BBC. Her poem 'Letter from Egypt' was featured in the Salvation Army's Christmas concert in the Royal Albert Hall, 2018.

For Fiona and Jen,
for Norman,
in memory of Allen
and for Ian with thanks

Some of these poems have been previously published by Indigo Dreams Press and Poetry Space. 'Broken Morning' was published by the RSPB.

Contents

Songbirds

No matter how hard you try,
ears periscoped to the skies,
some secrets are known
only to songbirds.

They hoard the music
of morning deep
in their throats until the sun
rubs sleep from his eyes.

Like kids, keeping gobs
of gum, stickers, pebbles
in trouser pockets, songbirds
store secrets in their wingtips.

Ghosts of the air, they
follow unseen maps, soar
on thermals, keeping knowledge
of flight to themselves, secret

as their morning song-sheets.

Broken morning

A blackbird
scrapes
the lightening sky
with knives of song,
wounds emptiness
with the lacerations
of its first
bleak notes.

The blackbird
sharpens
nightlong coldness
on a strop of frost,
whets loneliness
with its pale music
and I half-hear
a remembered voice.

Canned morning

birds cut into
the sky, easing
off the lid
with tin-openers
of song

the can of dawn
brims over, spills
colour, reds, crimsons,
glorious golds across
the dark

every bird
in every tree
empties its throat
of music, trills,
chirps, burbles, caws

with gay abandon
pouring sunshine
over the new day,
urging us
to mop it up, glorying

in a riot of song

New every morning

Sunshine,
new every morning
is ancient as the world
it shines on.

Hard to believe
that every person
who's ever lived has shared
its yellow heat.

You waken, part
curtains, peer through
the blinds, A lovely day
perfect for drying shirts.

My grandmother stood
at the back door, I remember,
her wetted forefinger forecasting
another sunny day.

In those days, summer
was always hot as hell,
the sun, new every morning,
flaunting its old-time shine

day after yellow day.

The day and the bird

It was his day
you could tell,
his song ripping up
the early hours
peeling back
frost, melting ice.

He stood tall
on the garden fence
opened his beak,
a yellow slash
in the dawn light
and sang, voice sharp

as silver scissors.

That first kiss

I was flattered, Ian *Boyd?*
Briggs? Bryce? (his name
started with a B, I'm sure)
— he'd invited me to see
his record collection —
me, out of all the girls
who fancied him, no wonder
I had a spring in my step.

Dark-haired, Brylcreemed
within an inch of his life,
he looked handsome
in blazer and school tie —
and he knew it — oh,
he knew it all right.
His voice had deepened,
and he'd started to shave.

He had his own attic room
done up with shelves, a sofa
and brand-new record player.
His vast collection featured
40's film stars, glossy covers
in black and white. I gazed
at them in awe. *Choose,*
he urged me. I couldn't.

So he grabbed me, bent me
backwards and kissed me
on the mouth. I hadn't expected
wet lips, tongue and spit. I gagged,
overbalanced and landed full

on a pile of his 78s. I heard
them crack. He swore,
dropped me like a hot cake —

a first unforgettable kiss.

Paint box

(For Norman)

I never met this man
owner of the Masonic box,
no longer around when his son
and I got together, but
he sounds quite a character.

Not that the box was used
as a paint box in his day,
no, then it held Masonic secrets
(like my grandfather — I wonder
where his box ended up?)

His son opens the lid, tubes
of half-squeezed oils lie
shoulder to shoulder, exotic
names reduced to numbers, brushes
lining the bottom of the box

Naples Yellow is No. 29, Cadmium
617, Chrome Yellow, 622 — a
whole new language for artists
to learn as they squeeze the last
drops from plastic tubes.

Ideal for the original owner who
must have been a numbers man
(he built and mended roads). Did
he ever imagine the riot of colour,
the landscapes, portraits, abstracts
his old box would one day hold?

The dancer

She's red-haired, a happy child
with a wicked sense of humour,
despite a mum who spends nights
in shiny satin and short skirts
with men of dubious background
and a need for sexual pleasure.

She's profoundly deaf, lip-reads
at speed, hangs an amplifier
on her chest. Her teachers wear
radio microphones — and sometimes
forget to switch off, causing laughter,
gales of laughter in the playground.

A gaggle of girls gathering
round her, pointing and giggling
alerts the staffroom — their secrets,
swear words, our candid comments
relayed top volume to an avid audience,
until the switch is flicked.

This deaf child's a talented dancer,
always in step, feet always in time,
the mainstay of Mrs Ayton's
country dance team. *How does she do it?*
we ask. She gazes in amazement.
I hear through my feet, of course!

Doesn't everyone?

(Mum has never seen her daughter dance)

Watching eyes

It's an honour, my mother said.
We'd been invited to Great Hall
for the afternoon, dropped off
by car.
                    Greeted by the
lady-of-the-house herself, we were
ushered into a dark hallway, curved
staircases, portraits on every wall
staring at me from grim painted eyes.

Margaret Rose! the lady called,
Meet your new little friend.
A pale child in a too-large kilt
and Fair Isle jersey reluctantly
acknowledged me. *Show her
your playroom*, her mother
ordered as mine was whisked off
to take tea.
                    I followed
the silent child to the top
of the house. She opened the door
to a huge half-empty room
with barred windows.
                    *Great grandmother's
dolls' house*, the girl said, unlocking
the old-fashioned toy, every room
peopled with beautifully- dressed
dolls, the size of a child's finger.
I reached into the kitchen where
the cook wore a tiny white apron.

Don't touch! My hostess was appalled
at my temerity.
I looked round —
a rocking horse, as tall as a pony
and a pile of wooden bricks,
the only toys in that vast room.
Mutely, we took
refuge in books, under the watchful
eyes of long-dead children whose
portraits lined the walls.
A maid in apron
and frilly cap brought us mugs of
hot milk (which I hate) and dry
shortbread biscuits. At last we were released.
I'm sure Moira
had a wonderful time, my mother
gushed. She nudged me, *Thank you*,
I managed as we left for the waiting car,
followed by the ever-watchful eyes
of the portraits on the walls.

Gran's house

In my head
I can wander through
Gran's house, going
from room to room in silent
easily-remembered footfalls.

A sunny porch
over the front steps,
(where we used to play houses
with miniature tea-cups
and clear lemonade).

Off the hall,
the front parlour, fat settees,
wind-up gramophone, palm in a pot
by the window and a coal fire
lit only on special occasions.

Next, the store room, a walk-through
to the kitchen where Gran
was Queen, a popping gas stove,
a stand of pots and pans
and the smell of cinnamon.

Then the back parlour,
heart of the house, long table,
easy chairs, the corner press
where Gran kept treacle toffees,
Grandpa his Masonic secrets.

Upstairs, the bathroom,
(old-fashioned as tea), my
grandparents' room, pink quilt
on the bed, mirrored dressing table
and Gran's earring box with drawers.

I remember a box-room
piled high with brown leather cases,
and best of all, a single bedroom
over the front door, all mine —
except for Gran who sat in sunshine

listening to me read my stories.

Unlocked

Murrayfield
a dawdle along Rose Street
drinks in every other pub
lights glinting on wet cobblestones
a late supper for four
jazz on CDs
smoochy dancing
a languorous stolen kiss
(to my embarrassment).

Next morning
Buck's Fizz with breakfast
(a luxury new to us)
the wife full of bonhomie
the man's grey eyes
following my every step
his hand on mine
just a little bit longer than usual —
a quiet journey home.

A day or so passes
the phone rings,
the guy from last weekend
When can I see you?
Flustered, I hesitate,
But I'm married. So?
What's that got to do
with anything? I can't
get you out of my mind.

Nothing comes of it,
(I'm too naïve, too married
to get involved), but
the offer unlocks
a new confidence
in me. Married or not,
I'm still a woman —
and surprise, surprise,
a sexy one at that.

On the edge of the sky

sitting
on the edge of the sky
dusting sand
from between my toes
perspectives shift
move out of kilter
and my eyes ache

in the blue-black light
I make out swallows
jitterbugging
beneath me
notched wings
outstretched

the tops of trees
huddling like mushrooms
ripe for picking
roads and rivers
hedges and ditches
parcelling the earth
into lots

grey rain collecting
belly-heavy
in cloud-balloons
about to burst

dizzy, I cling
to tufts of rank grass
and sea thrift
to shadows of childhood

as I search the air
for something
I didn't know

I'd lost

Daffodils

Yellow on yellow
starring the grass
in groups
like teenagers
gossiping together,
whispering, giggling.

Yellow on yellow
searing the eyes
as they huddle
face-to-face
two bunches to a vase
on the breakfast table.

They smell sharp
of promise, of spring
one day open-mouthed
glowing, the next
crumpled, spent,
yellow on yellow

yesterday's brilliance.

The prurient wind

Leaves lift petticoats, their tender
unmentionables on show,
autumn roses undulate
undressing petal by petal,
veil by veil.

Grasses bend in submission, hair
in disarray, knickers in a twist,
lecherous birds rubbernecking
from vantage points
in the sky.

Waves tug off their jodhpurs,
leap astride silver horses, roar
full-throated, lusting after
stones lying vulnerable
on the shore.

Signatures

Winter trees
carve their names
in deep black script
on the reddening sky,

blot spreading ink
with frayed
fist-held edges
of spit-grey cloud

willows sign in slow
languid strokes
oaks in a childish hand
sycamore in haste

putting their mark
on the season's skies
before spring blurs
the clarity of names

with burgeoning green.

Mother moon

The moon
is the mother of sadness,
hanging alone in the night
wet handkerchief
balled in her hand.

She squints
at the world through
tear-smeared spectacles
and, sobbing hugely,
calls angels to her side.

They have
better things to do
with themselves, *Give over,*
dear, they say, *you're not*
the only widow woman!

Without ceremony
they heave her into space
to keen unseen, unheard.
Earthlings huddle
in the unaccustomed dark.

What the devil's
going on? Wings whirring,
the angel horde relents,
hooks Mother Moon to a star,
births a baby — their proper job.

Sleepless night

Perhaps
watching the World Cup
was too much for him,
perhaps
it was the second glass
of whisky
in celebration,
maybe it was
the sticky
highly unusual heat

Whatever the cause
he couldn't sleep,
chatted on about penalties
(as if I cared)
and who missed what.
We kissed
made love
each popping to the loo
settled down
or so we thought.

Night unrolled
into minutes, hours,
we checked the time.
He got up,
watched more football
made toast
and Horlicks.
I got up, topped up
my orange juice
from the fridge

‘How about
a burst of Kindle?’
he asked.
We chose
a Mary Wesley
we’d heard before.
I opted
in and out of the story.
It finished,
all seven hours of it,
at 8.30 am.

I gave up
loitered in
a much-needed shower.
Sitting over breakfast,
we reviewed the story
filling in the bits
each had heard
our eyes prickling
with loss of sleep.
World Cup?
Who cares? Not me.

In the dark

The dark is a different dimension.
Crows' wings, deep-dug mines,
leafless winter trees come to mind.

Yet we look to the skies at night,
revelling in the silver of stars,
the magic of a full moon, planets.

The dark is a constant, always
otherworldly, filled with wonder
as earth-bound eyes gaze upwards.

It swirls its magic cloak, black on
black, dimming starlight, blurring clouds,
blocking the promised blue moon.

The dark is a mysterious dimension.

Good-night, sweetheart

Sounds good
when he says it
as he turns over
and he's lost
until the alarm trills
at 8 next morning
and he's capable
of movement,
a whiskery kiss
and you switch on
Radio 4.

You think about
where you've been
all these dark hours,
where he's been
come to that,
close, sweaty-hot
but unreachable
in dreamtime,
a stranger
in your bed,
unknowable
as any other man
in the street.

Stillness

Trees
baring their bones
in the run-up
to winter's austerity
loan
their slight
distortions
to the magic mirror
of a languid lake
capturing
the very essence
of stillness.

Winter sunlight

Shadows are long and lean
and very black
making their hand-in-hand way
along a sunlit road.

They mingle and two-step
with tree shapes
twisting and twirling
to the music of a blue wind.

A clear white-cold light
scars the eyes, blinding
the staid walkers as, slowly,
they re-trace Strictly steps.

They remember Balling
the Jack, long-gone nights
in black tie, long black frocks,
hearts and feet in perfect time.

Now they shadow-dance with
black trees, keeping in step,
jiving, waltzing, fox-trotting
into the shimmer of winter.

The hurricane

wraps his dark blue coat
round thin shoulders
steps into the forest
wrecking-ball breath at the ready
planting size 12 boots
all over ferns and tangled roots
tearing at the highest branches
with long black finger nails

he sings in a low baritone
a song full of menace, of threat
leaving a trail of destruction
in his wake — unsatisfied, he turns
his attention to stone walls, to
roof-tiles and garden fences,
his coat swirling, feet trampling
parked cars, bollards, traffic lights;

in high good humour he dances
a macabre dance, twirling and
spinning to a rhythm of his own
and laughs out loud, pulls his
mobile from an inside pocket
takes selfies posing arrogantly
by the debris of a village school
before retreating to gloat over
          such successful havoc
                    from his base
                              far above the clouds.

Thunder in the mountains

like iron-shod racehorses
galloping towards
the finish, manes blowing
wild in the wind

like a crowd jostling, restive
in some faraway square,
eager to hear the leader's
words of promise

like sky-giants swearing,
shouting insults
while hurling closed-fist
punches at one another

until the sun relents,
tempers calm down,
horses whinny, crowds
wave jubilant flags in the air

and mountains heave a sigh
of relief.

Going solo
(Swallows mate for life)

He haunts
the telephone wire,
assiduous, patient
perched neatly
as a crochet
on a song sheet.

He opens his beak
and sings, voice
robust as ever
filling the evening air
with hope, with
a terrible sadness.

Each call ends
in the same
tremulous trill,
loneliness
in every last
piercing note.

He gives stray
females the push
as he waits
for his one-and-only
singing his songs
of incredible longing.

Sparrows and chips

Waves lick the shore
sun spills from a cloudless sky
as we sip drinks, he a beer,
me pink wine, the beach umbrella
drawing circles of shadow
          on the sand.

I have my usual, avocado
and shrimps. He orders chips,
sprinkles them with salt
and vinegar, eats, savouring
every mouthful. Sparrows
on flypast calculate
          his appetite.

He throws the odd chip
into the air. Birds vie
with one another to catch
tidbits on the wing. We watch
the acrobatic display, soak up
          sunshine, rock music

and the sound of the sea.

Your hands

You wrap your hands
around me like silver ribbons,
touch my skin with fingertips
cool as liquid drops.

You make music
with those same hands
drawing jazz melodies
like magic from the air.

You have long-ago
builder's hands, capable,
once strong — once artist's hands
creating pots from clay.

Now they are arthritic, knotty,
but you finger my cheek,
and they're soft as magnolia petals
and as beautiful.

Frangipani

One of the things
I've dreamed of, candidate
for my bucket list -

a man offering me
flowers for my hair -
perhaps with a kiss?

Last night my dreams
came true - a young man
gave me a spray of flowers,

fragrant frangipani, white
waxy petals, moon-yellow
centre, golden stamens.

For your hair; he said.
Instead of a kiss (I'm
past my sell-by date)

he took a hand-held selfie.

Just sitting

We sit in the garden,
the last of the May sunshine
filtering through
maple and copper beech.

We sip iced G&Ts,
listen to the blackbird,
to the fountain tiptoeing
into the pond.

We've planted boxfuls
of geraniums and begonias
in clay pots, sweated over
the unaccustomed exercise.

Now in the cool
of the evening, we relax
in one another's company,
happy to be together,

just sitting.

Imagine a kiss

Imagine a kiss,
he says, voice thick
impeded
by an oxygen mask.
You think
of a lifetime's
kisses, warm
wet baby kisses,
inexpert skidding-
across-the-mouth
teenage kisses,
of those
more ardent
more experienced
the man-to-woman
exploring sort.
You remember
bedtimes,
confident
husband-to-wife
Good-night, sleep-well
kisses, knowing
tomorrow would come,
until the day
tomorrow failed
and a run-of-the-mill kiss
morphed into the last,
a dead man's
kiss.

Lunch in the sun

For weeks
we thought nothing of it,
loaded a tray
with cheese and chutney
bananas and biscuits and beer
sat in the shade
beneath a red umbrella.
It became a way of life.

We listened
to the gentle burble
of fountain into pond,
watched butterflies
flirt in the sunshine,
sipped wine (me) beer (you)
filed the fierce heat
in a folder marked

in bold type, SUMMER 2018.

All of me

You take my all,
every snatch of skin,
every eager fingertip,
every sigh of satisfaction
and yet, I'm all alone
in the end. Everyone is,
no matter how close.

You sing, *All of me*,
but you lie. You must.
Yes, you know every inch
of my body, from toes
upwards, every inflection
of my voice. You know me
from the outside in.

You keep your memories
in a private place, under
lock and key — as do I.
Some parts of me are
foreign territory to you
where your passport is
of no possible use.

All of me is a nice idea,
but we live and dream
alone, our thoughts
not ours to share — unlike
breakfast, the duvet,
a hot shower. I am yours
on the outside, inside
I'm my own woman.

It felt like flowers

High summer,
a tartan rug
strawberries bought
from a market stall
wine cooled
in the languid stream,
Thank God
for the invention
of screw-tops,
he said, pouring
white wine
into plastic tumblers.

Picnic over
we sprawled
barely breathing
beneath leaf-heavy
trees, mapping
the sense
of one another
lingering over
this one final
precious hour.
I closed my eyes
to white-hot heat.

I wore a long cotton
skirt, rucked up
to my thighs,
he a shirt unbuttoned
to the waist. We relived
our four nights

in one bed, shared
conversations
to last a lifetime.
His fingers explored
my limbs, my hair,
my exhausted face.

It felt like flowers.

Telltale touch

His sleeping hand
on my thigh
is enough,

tells me
everything
I need to know,

speaks of trust,
of easy familiarity,
of lazy love-making

waiting in the wings.

Pretty woman

Age doesn't matter
nor a dodgy leg
when a pretty woman
pushes past,
his deep-down instinct
galvanised
into action.

His eyes relish
the bouncy hair,
long slim legs,
the perky breasts,
follow her confident progress
along the street.

Delighted to say
I'm not dead yet,
he smiles, taking
my hand in his
as we make for the car,
the woman long gone
from sight, leaving behind

one fluttering heart.

Flamingo feathers

In a dusty envelope
clearly labelled
in her neat writing,
Flamingo feathers —
true, a fistful
of almost weightless pink
floats from its hiding place.

Had she been
to visit the zoo?
Did she pick them up
one by one at the salt-flats
birds on stilt-high legs
looking on? Did
the children find them?

So much I don't know
about this woman
whose man, whose bed
I share. She was exotic,
very beautiful, in portraits
watchful, always young.

If I should find a feather
on the front path,
it's likely to be a sparrow's
or at best from
a blackbird's inky tail,
nothing exciting.

Maybe next time
my luck will hold and I'll find
a glorious multi-coloured
peacock feather — now that
would take some beating
in the exoticism stakes.

Grandfather

Let me help you,
the young man says
taking the older man's arm
as they climb the steep steps
to a neighbour's house.

You are my grandfather;
he jokes — but there's
a serious tone to his words.
To us, we're getting on,
although *old* is for others.

We know we're not as spry
as we once were, but
we're not really old, not us.
Youngsters view us differently —
to them, we're positively doddery.

So maybe we should sit back
let them help, take over.
One day, in a future they
can't imagine, they too will
use sticks, need spectacles,

be Grandma and Grandfather.

Finding out

I wonder
what dying is like —
different
for everyone perhaps,
but the way I feel
I guess
I'll soon find out.

Somehow
I'm not in charge
of myself,
no appetite, dizzy,
frequent trips to the loo,
a headache
Nurofen doesn't touch.

As the poet says,
Days are where we live
so I'm living today,
feeling better, but still
wondering, still giving death
the odd thought.
I'll find out soon enough

no doubt. Watch this space.

Heartsease

I've heard of wearing
hearts on your sleeve
the heart of the matter
a heart-to-heart talk
but lying snug
beneath a satin heart
is something else.

I've heard of *Heartsease*
small broken hearts
spreading purple and yellow
among the stones
but who thought up
their nickname
Jack-jump-up-and-kiss-me?

And of course I know
how two hearts can beat
in the jazzed-up rhythms
of love-making —
beneath an open window
heart-shaped flowers
reflect on their other name

Come-and-cuddle-me.

Searching for the second magpie

Maple branches sing into green
and one bird of joy, flaunting its
zebra feathers, zips to the place
        where tree meets sky.

Not a great omen — so what's
new? You've learned to live with
the oneness of things, one plate,
        one mug, one glass.

You turn from the window, shrug,
That old wives' tale! — but your
eyes strain for a flash of matching
        jet-bright wings.

Your ring catches the sun — with
a sorcerer's timing, the perfect pair
strut across the grass, splendid in
        full evening dress.

Kleptomaniacs, these two — gold has
done the trick. If only it were as easy
to conjure up the one person who
        could change your life.

The colour of fear

Fear waves its flag
in my face,
so near, so close,
I can't make out
its true colours.

A strident orange?
Fierce blood-red
banners streaking
across my eyes?
Old-lady purple?

The doctor hammers
on a keyboard, gazes
at his computer screen.
*We'll get to the bottom
of this*, he says, smiling.

I try to divert him
with talk of Murrayfield —
no such luck. He turns,
holding the fear flag
in both hands, unfurls it.

He pats my shoulder
(the painful one), says
It will be OK. I grab
the flag, its rainbow stripes
fluttering in the cold air.

Its lurid colours terrify me.

Persephone's daughters

They live their own lives, these
daughters. They must. OK, so
their spring was yours, but you
had to let them go — to fall out
of trees, off wobbling bicycles.

Skinned knees made better
with a kiss, a Band-Aid, a toffee —
easy it was, in those snowdrop days.
Turn your back and spring's become
summer, celandines are sunflowers.

And you, in your copper-leaved coat
must remain silent as they fall in and
out of love, their tears tearing holes in
your eyes. No pomegranates for them —
they take knives to unripe lemons.

When the autumn sun rides high,
you gather the scattered pips, poke them
into pots on the greenhouse shelf. You
pour wine, make cups of scalding coffee
and look forward to the white of winter.

Poacher's pocket

We keep secrets
locked in deep pockets
inside our winter coats.

Like poachers, we
hide them away, afraid
of exposure to daylight,

to prying ears and eyes.
In the dark of night
while lovers sleep

we prise open pockets,
unravel memories one by one,
bringing them back to life,

before a return to their hiding-place
in the thick tweed coat hanging
on its hook behind the door.

News from Glasgow

I didn't quite
catch it, Liz Lochead
on Radio 4,

something about
fires and the bravery
of firemen.

She couldn't
believe what
had happened,

I couldn't
make out what
she was talking about.

News headlines,
Fire in Glasgow's
School of Art,

the famous
Mackintosh building —
I walked past it

every day
on my way to school.
I couldn't believe it

either — not again!

Seeing water

We can't yet see
the water
hearing only
its restlessness
fingering weed
making pathways
over stones
under rocks
till a tumble
of unstoppable movement
fragments streams
into a froth of droplets.

We feel the spray
gentling the summer air
taunting cheeks
diamond-beading hair
drawing us
towards the grandeur
of purest white
on black — water
in all its thunderous glory
bouncing, cascading, plunging —
like seeing water
for the very first time.

Frosted glass

The pattern lives
in my left eye,
the damaged one.

Spots and bubbles
overlay faces, branches,
bus numbers, M&S shelves.

Like an old flag,
tattered at the edges,
it flutters on my sight-line.

It's dreary, off-white
lacking in imagination,
I'd prefer something colourful,

but I've no say in the matter.
I look through my opaque window,
only too glad to recognise

his bearded face, close-up.

Ghost practice

Sometimes I practise my ghost-life,
wear my skin inside-out, vulnerable
to touch, to the wrong word
being spoken. I'm not good at it,
need more practice, try to get out
of it by swallowing two Nurofen.

My reflection in a sunlit mirror flags up
every imperfection, wrinkles, fading
hair colour, floppy arms. I'm on my way
to ghost-hood but can't accept it. I dye
my hair, rub creams into my face, almost
believing their magic anti-aging powers.

True, I expect my tomorrows to come,
wash, iron & fold away tees for next time,
chop melon into mouth-size cubes,
cut up grapes, cover, ready for a breakfast
that might not come — well not for me
at least. Do ghosts eat fruit for breakfast?

Paper bird

It swings
with the slight breeze
from an open window,
flying on a cotton strand
almost invisible
to the naked eye.

Silently it sways
to the mood music
of a blackbird's
yellow morning call,
twirls, restless on
its restraining thread.

Like those women
caught in long-dead
marriage bonds
longing to test
paper wings
on the outside world.

A blind woman's poem

They expect it to be
in black and white,
the odd grey phrase
to suggest texture — no,
not for this woman.
She goes for colour
in a big way, exulting
in glorious reds,
luminous blues,
luscious greens.

She paints her poems
with some subtlety,
remembering the faces
of daffodils
smiling their open
golden smiles, primroses
hiding their paleness
among spring grasses,
the rush of blue
in shy forget-me-nots.

Her clear blind eyes
work with a palette
of peacock oils
scattering colour
across her words,

taking on Jackson Pollock
at his own game,
rivalling Van Gogh
with his blues and golds
whirling in a night sky.

Colour? The blind poet
has no fear of over-doing it.

Died of wounds

Funny, no-one talked about him.
Not much anyway, his nephew says,
They say he shot down a Zeppelin
but we don't know if this is true.

He shows me the sepia photograph
of a soldier, young, a little stern,
none too sure of himself, but clutching
his newly acquired officer's baton.

Three years in France, years of shells
and mud and fear, until the message,
Regret to inform you, Lt. H Leater
died of wounds on 22nd March 1918,

six months before the guns fell silent,
only 25 years old. The King signed
the letter of condolence — not by hand,
of course. So many deaths, too many

to sign his name in ink time after time.

The all-alone blues
(For Norman)

No gigs,
just a single trumpet
practising the music
of old New Orleans,
a lone voice
singing the blues.

No choice,
a few bleak notes
on the solo trumpet
a melancholy,
a lonely voice singing
of stormy weather
of blues in the rain.

No clarinet,
no piano or bass,
no trombone or sax,
just one trumpet,
the music making
a macabre beauty

all of its own.

Teach your child to fly

Hold your baby up
high enough
to see the moon,
watch silver stars
dancing in the dark.

Tell him he can fly
with wings made
from night-time dreams
colours streaking like
ribbons across the sky.

Tell him about castles
in the air,
of dragons, of unicorns
standing proud and tall
in the depths of a forest.

Make sure he knows
how to take off
travelling across continents
in his imagination,
no passport required.

Show him how
to land safely
storing magic in his bags
to ward off
the drudgery of everyday.

Teach your child to fly
in dreamtime
and he'll grow up rich
rattling poems like gold pennies
deep in his pockets.

Squeezed like loneliness

space filled to the brim
with spider-whiteness
no bird call
no knock on the door
loneliness
squeezed into a corner
like a hunted animal
waiting
waiting for the phone to ring
for a voice on the other end
of the line
email doesn't do it
nor Facebook
nor Linked-in
loneliness needs
its own space and time
excelling in taunting
with borrowed laughter
from across the street
the sight of hand on hand
on a Sainsbury's trolley
a stranger's accidental touch
his words of apology
like the last drops of loneliness
squeezed from a wash-rag

God made woman

He gave her lips to kiss,
hair to tangle with,
a hidden cleft
just made to fit.

Men fondle her
promise undying love,
whisper in her ear, lying,
they hold her close.

They call her Low-down
woman, exploit her,
love her, leave her
belly full of baby.

Obviously God is a man.

Too many oceans in your song

The dreamscape
of deep blue waters
is all-embracing.
I try to swim (I'm
a good swimmer)
float with the tide
imagine I might drown.

You stand on the shore
your voice deep, true
singing the blues
of downtown streets
in old New Orleans
of getting the blues
when it rains. Stop!

What about me?
I call, my voice thin
wavering in the wind
as the ocean sucks me
down into blues like
you've never known,
indigo, peacock, sapphire.

And still you sing
the blues of rundown streets,
Bourbon, Beale, Basin …
Even the smooth red tiles
of a Tin Roof turn blue.

You ignore my struggles
in the ocean's blue depths.
Too many deepdown dreams,
too many oceans in your song.

Absence

I knew he’d be back.
I felt his breath
in the wind
saw his reflection
in the waters
of the sluggish stream.

His fingers twisted
the topmost branches —
he’d been a tall man —
and all mine,
heartbeats in synch
as we lay in bed.

I heard his voice
singing jazz solos
under a white moon,
his top trumpet notes
among the stars.
I waited in silence

for his touch, one
finger’s worth on my lips,
knowing he’d promised
to return one more time,
I waited, better waited —
no luck. These days

is absence his presence?
Another way of listening?

Don’t just use your ears.
Absorb music through your skin.
Listen with your heart.

Holding on to music

sometimes
it reverberates
unwanted
inside your head,
lyrics and tunes going
round and round

sometimes
it drives you
up the wall
and sleep escapes
as you grasp at
a song's ragged edges

sometimes
you get lucky
music becoming
just a soundtrack
to deepest dreams
like a lullaby from
long-lost years ago.

Almost

I almost met you
glimpsed you across the street
looking in the window
of an antiques shop,
(*typical,* I thought)
I stepped into the road,
an impatient horn
drawing me back
and I missed you.

What would I have said?
I'm happily married …
Might you have asked, 'Love him?'
I loved him to bits, would have
told you so, but he was ill,
waiting for me to drive him
to hospital. I'd rushed out
to buy the Guardian, sandwiches
and fruit for the journey.

You'd have greeted me
with a kiss, long and hard
right there on High Street,
suggested coffee, a drink,
keen to catch up, to know
I was OK. Too late, no time.
You merged into the crowd.
I remembered your grey eyes,
the salty smell of you.

I almost met you.

And suddenly

And suddenly
the sun is shining
colour seeps back
into the garden
its sleeping face
not quite sure
what's happening
rubbing its eyes
as it searches
for answers.

And just as suddenly
the sky pales
slow tears leak
from shuttered lids
questions answered
fair and square —
What do you expect?
This is England
where rain follows sun
as night shadows day.